KU-430-608

GO FACTS PLANTS

Trees

A & C BLACK • LONDON

Trees

contents

© Blake Publishing Pty Ltd 2002
Additional Material © A & C Black Publishers Ltd 2003

First published 2002 in Australia by Blake Education Pty Ltd

This edition published 2003 in the United Kingdom by
A&C Black Publishers Ltd, 37 Soho Square, London W1D 3QZ
www.acblack.com

Published by permission of Blake Publishing Pty Ltd, Glebe NSW, Australia.
All rights reserved. No part of this publication may be reproduced in any
form or by any means – graphic, electronic or mechanical, including
photocopying, recording, taping or information storage and retrieval
systems – without the prior written permission of the publishers.

ISBN 0-7136-6596-3

A CIP record for this book is available from the British Library.

Written by Paul McEvoy
Science Consultant: Dr Will Edwards, School of Tropical Biology, James
Cook University
Design and layout by The Modern Art Production Group
Photos by Photodisc, Stockbyte, John Foxx, Corbis, Imagin,
Artville and Corel

UK Series Consultant: Julie Garnett

Printed in Hong Kong by Wing King Tong Co Ltd

A & C Black uses paper produced with elemental chlorine-free pulp,
harvested from managed sustainable forests.

ISLINGTON LIBRARIES	
LIBRARY & ACC. No.	S.
CLASS No.	582.16
CATG'D	DATE

What is a Tree?

A tree is a plant with a tall, woody trunk. Like all plants, trees need air, water and sunlight to live and grow.

A tree has a long, woody trunk covered in bark. The trunk supports the branches, lifting them high above the ground. Bark is dead and protects the living trunk inside. The trunk grows thicker and taller each year.

Trees have many branches. Tree branches spread out in all directions toward sunlight. More and more branches grow each year.

Leaves grow on the branches. The leaves cover the tree in a canopy of green. Leaves use the sun's energy to make food for the whole tree.

The tree has roots under the ground. Roots **absorb** water and nutrients from the soil. Trees need water to live and grow. The roots also hold the tree firm when the wind blows.

leaves

branch

trunk

roots under the ground

A tree has a trunk, branches, leaves and roots.
Each part of a tree is important.

Life Cycle of a Tree

Trees are alive. Like all living things, trees grow, change and reproduce. Even the largest trees start life as small seeds.

1 The life of a new tree starts when a seed drops from a branch. It may drop to the ground or be carried away by an animal, by wind or by water. A seed needs water and warmth to begin to grow.

2 Small roots grow down into the ground to reach for water. A green shoot grows up into the sunlight. The young tree must begin to make its own food.

3 Young trees are called saplings. Saplings grow straight and tall towards sunlight.

4 When the tree is mature it flowers. New seeds grow from the flowers.

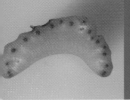

How Do Trees Drink Water?

Trees take in water through their roots. How does the water get all the way up to the top of the tree?

Try this experiment.

What you need:

- fresh celery
- glass jar
- food colouring (red works well)

What to do:

1 Use a stalk of celery with leaves. Cut off the end.

2 Pour a small amount of food colouring into the glass jar. Place the celery in the food colouring.

3 Place the jar in a sunny spot and wait 15 minutes.

4 Cut the celery into sections. How far has the colour moved up the stem?

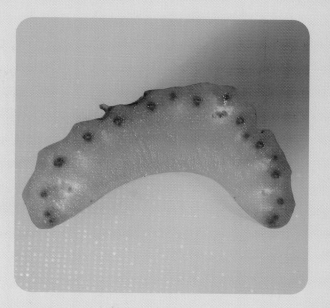

Food colouring moves up the celery stalk through strawlike tubes.

The celery stalk is standing in food colouring.

The food colouring has reached the leaves.

9

Types of Trees

Trees come in many shapes and sizes. All trees can be grouped into three main types. These are conifers, palms and broadleaf trees.

Conifers

Conifer trees have tall, straight trunks and thin, spiky leaves or needles. The tough, needle-shaped leaves can survive very cold winters and heavy snow. Most conifers are **evergreen** trees that do not lose their leaves in winter.

Conifer trees make their seeds inside cones. Pines, firs and cedar trees are all conifers.

conifer forest

pine cone

10

coconut palms

Palms

Palm trees have straight trunks without branches. The long palm leaves grow from the top of the trunk. Palm leaves are shaped like feathers or fans.

All palm trees grow seeds inside a fruit. Some palm trees grow fruit that people can eat. Coconuts and dates are palm fruits that people use for food.

date palms

11

Broadleaf trees

Most **species** of tree are **broadleaf trees**. They often have flat, wide leaves.

Big, flat leaves can catch lots of sunlight but they need lots of water. Some broadleaf trees are **deciduous** and lose their leaves in winter. Oak, horse chestnut and beech trees all drop their leaves in winter.

Broadleaf evergreen trees, such as holly and orange trees, grow in warmer areas. They do not lose their leaves. These trees have thicker, waxy leaves that often contain oil. The leaves can be large, small, long or short.

Broadleaf trees are flowering plants. New seeds grow from the flowers. Some seeds are carried by wind or water to new places. Others are wrapped in a fruit which animals might carry away.

Oak trees
are deciduous.

Orange trees
are evergreen.

The leaves of deciduous trees
change colour in autumn.

Trees and Seasons

In cold climates, most broadleaf trees lose their leaves in winter. The short, cold days cause the leaves to fall. Trees that lose their leaves in winter are called deciduous trees.

Spring

1

As the weather warms up, the tree buds and new leaves grow. The tree may also flower.

14

Summer

2

The tree grows. A green covering of leaves creates food for the whole tree.

Autumn

3

As the weather begins to cool, and days grow shorter, the food moves from the leaves to the trunk and roots. Leaves lose their green colour and become dry and brittle. When the leaves are dead, they fall from the tree.

Winter

4

During winter, a deciduous tree stops growing. The tree is still alive. It is waiting for warm temperatures before it starts to grow again.

Forests

A forest is a place where many trees grow together. Forests cover more than one-quarter of the land on Earth. There are many different types of forests, from pine forests to rainforests.

Trees usually grow together, forming forests. All plants need sunlight and tall trees get lots of sunshine. Having their leaves high above the ground helps to protect trees from hungry animals.

pine forest

Trees can live in many different areas, but the higher the rainfall the more trees will grow.

Tropical rainforests grow in the hot, wet areas near the **Equator**. These rainforests are filled with a wide variety of evergreen broadleaf trees. Brazil's Amazon rainforest is the largest rainforest in the world.

This is a tropical
rainforest in Brazil.

Rainforests also grow
in temperate areas.

17

Trees adapt to their environment.

Conifer trees grow in vast areas just below the North Pole. Snow covers these huge conifer forests for many months of the year. The hardy conifer tree with its tough needles does well in these cold areas.

eucalyptus

Temperate forests grow where the weather is milder. These places have four to six months of warm to hot summers. A variety of trees grow in these areas. In California, temperate forests are made up of giant redwood trees. Oaks and maples grow in temperate deciduous forests. Eucalyptus tree forests are common in Australia.

pine forest

18

towering
redwood trees

GO FACTS

DID YOU KNOW?
The Wollemi pine trees in Australia are 'living fossils'. They were growing when dinosaurs were alive.

Trees as Homes

Many animals live in trees. Trees provide food and shelter for monkeys, squirrels, birds and insects.

Most monkeys find food and shelter in trees. They can also escape from land-based predators to their homes above the ground. Monkeys are well-adapted to life in the trees. Their tails help them to climb and leap from branch to branch.

Many small mammals live in trees. Trees provide shelter from wind, rain and other animals. Holes in trees become homes for squirrels and acorns are their food. In Australia, koalas live and feed in eucalyptus trees.

koala

Many birds live their lives in trees. They build their nests in the branches or hollows of trees. Trees provide fruit, nectar and seeds for birds to eat.

Millions of insects live in trees. Many types of beetles, ants and butterflies depend on trees for food and shelter.

Raccoons often build their dens in hollow trees.

Gorillas are at home in trees.

Some birds build their nests in trees.

Trees, Flowers and Seeds

Type of tree	Does it flower?	Is it evergreen?	Where are the seeds?
coconut palm	yes	yes	coconut
oak	yes	no	acorn
pine	no	yes	pine cone
lemon	yes	yes	lemon
apricot	yes	no	apricot
holly	yes	yes	berry

Glossary

absorb	take in
broadleaf tree	a tree with branches and flat leaves
conifer	a tree with needle-shaped leaves and cones
deciduous	losing their leaves in winter
Equator	an imaginary line drawn around the centre of the Earth
evergreen	trees that keep their leaves all year
rainforest	a thick forest in a warm area where there is a lot of rain
species	a type or kind of living thing
temperate	area with moderate temperatures
tropical	being warm and wet enough for plants to grow all year round

Index